Manifesto:
Staffing Capitol Hill

Cathy Travis

DEDICATION

Dedicated to the men and women who work round the clock for lousy money to serve the public good on Capitol Hill. Others may not appreciate you, but I do.

CT

Special thanks to Liza Lynch

CONTENTS

ACKNOWLEDGMENTS

About the cover photo:

The cover photo underlying my book title was taken by U.S. Navy Chief Electronics Technician James Clark. It is a unique picture of the dome reflected in the water and glass over the Capitol Visitor's Center on the south side of the U.S. Capitol. The entire photo shows a worker putting a cover on it; you can still see his face in the reflection.

Thanks to the U.S. Navy for making this photo available; the following is from the United States Navy:
090111-N-9923C-778 WASHINGTON (Jan. 11, 2009)
"Mark Holland, from the Architect of the Capitol-Insulation Division, applies a protective covering to the skylights of the U.S. Capitol Visitor's Center to protect the glass from the propeller wash of the in-coming helicopter during the 56th Presidential Inauguration rehearsal in Washington. More than 5,000 men and women in uniform are providing military ceremonial support to the presidential inauguration, a tradition dating back to George Washington's 1789 inauguration. (U.S. Navy photo by Chief Electronics Technician James Clark/Released)"

*****

No information herein should be considered official, or be considered to accurately reflect the present law. It is not from the House of Representatives, nor is it meant as a substitute for legal advice to anybody.

*****

i

1. FROM THE AUTHOR

I worked on the Hill from 1983-2008, in several offices, with working relationships in hundreds of different offices, with varying political circumstances, in both the majority and the minority.

The constant similarity across the Hill – whatever the party, or evolving technologies, or political climate – is the desire for the office to be well run.

For Capitol Hill, that means knowing who does what, writing down the general rules, holding staffers accountable for their work, and planning (as much as possible for the Hill) in advance.

My very first job was a peon job working on the Floor of the House of Representatives. It was the best peon job ever.

Past that, I worked as a press secretary mostly, and a senior advisor later. I worked in – or advised – local and national political campaigns ... but mostly wrote press releases, speeches, and talked to reporters on Capitol Hill for 25 years.

It's said a bunch of different ways here, but every single office is different ... various circumstances, strength at different places on the staff, conditions in the district, political realities, money concerns, and a thousand other considerations or variations.

For all the similarities, every single office is different ... run as its own entity, and with various levels of talent on the team as people come and go.

Most offices have similar staff and concerns, so many times the information here is qualified as "most offices" or "generally" to reiterate that every single office does things their own way, for their own reasons.

Nobody else will tell you, in such candid detail, about the essence of working on Capitol Hill. It can be such a prestigious job, and all you really hear on the front end – besides it being a hard job to get and then keep – is the prestige and glory. Which there is in abundance ... but you don't start to get the full idea of how it's going to go until you are already in it.

Working on the Hill is unlike any other workplace in the nation.

This overview is in two parts. The first part is for interns or anybody new to the Hill to run through logistics and basic information. The second, more extensive, part is about the specifics of various jobs in a congressional office.

During my 25 years on the Hill, many people told me I should write a book about how to be a staffer, an idea I always laughed off as I ran through my day on Capitol Hill. But the suggestions kept coming after I left the Hill, since this information doesn't presently exist anywhere else.

Everybody who has come to work on the Hill has wished at some point they'd had – up front – good information about the context of the entire staff, and specific advice for how to do their job well.

The information here is nowhere near exhaustive, and isn't meant to be. It only skims the very top of the surface regarding how to operate in congressional staff jobs.

Whatever you are doing on the Hill, good luck and do it well. The experience will be one you talk about for the rest of your life.

- Cathy Travis

2. NEW TO THE HILL?

Capitol Hill is every bit as exciting – and mortifying – as you might have heard.   Regardless of your political party or office, there are some overarching similarities in all, or most, offices of the Members of Congress.

Every single office is run essentially as its own nonprofit – with its own budget and rules of operation.

Information here is qualified as "most offices" or "generally" to reiterate that every single office does things their own way, for their own reasons.

Congress consists of both the U.S. House of Representatives (HOR), and the U.S. Senate. While this guide is specifically written for the House side, nearly all the same dynamics hold true on the Senate side, too. But the Senate has fewer members, much larger staffs, and sometimes different sensibilities.

If you are a new intern, it helps very much to commit some basic information about your boss to memory; do it out of the office, and keep some office details where you can see it easily (recommend taping it near the phone).

The basic information can be found on office websites.

• Correct spelling of the Member's name,

• The number of the Congressional district, and exactly what part of the state the district includes,

• Phone, fax numbers, address for the D.C. office, and all district offices,

• What district offices correspond with what area (usually counties), and

• Read through recent press releases to get a flavor of what's been going on recently.

Many offices will give interns a briefing on arrival. But some are just too stacked up on the first day to give you a lot more information past, "sit here, and answer the phone." So do that and try to stay out of the way. Somebody will get to you to explain stuff, usually. If not, figure it out and watch what people do.

You're already coming to the party better prepared than others, by virtue of reading this pretty exhaustive overview.

The Washington staff generally handles issues considered by the House of Representatives each day, researching legislation, writing constituent responses on issues before Congress, conducting press strategy, and scheduling time for the Member of Congress.

District offices focus mostly on the Member's constituent services. They work primarily with federal, state or local agencies to resolve individual problems for people back home.

WHAT TO EXPECT

While in Washington, you will see the legislative process in the United States Congress, up close and personal. Be prepared for a fast-paced work environment that will require your careful attention, energy, and professionalism.

Intern assignments can range from running errands, clerical work and answering phones ... to giving Capitol tours or reporting on committee hearings ... to conducting legislative research or drafting correspondence.

Most offices do not pay interns; there's little need for that. There are internship programs that offices can take advantage of ... and the insight an intern gets on the Hill is an awfully valuable commodity, for college and eventually the workplace. There is usually an overabundance of young people wanting to intern for free.

While the Hill is full of characters – people who move and shape policy – interns are not yet among them. You are an intern. Context is everything in understanding your place in the pecking order and your actual value to the office.

Interns frequently expect they will be making national policy when they walk in the door. You are not. If you are lucky, you can help ... but first you have to prove yourself. It's not that hard, and consistency is pretty much demanded.

Here's how an intern can be helpful to an office:

• Be on time, every day. The further out you stay, the greater the chance the metro or traffic will have problems that delay you. So account for that on the front end. If you are remarkably early, read the morning publications in the cafeteria.

• Learn to answer the phone – what to say and how to transfer calls ... different staff members will be various levels of high maintenance about how they want calls delivered (a little more detail later).

• Ask how all staffers want calls delivered and consistently do it correctly. Most staffers won't use interns for research, writing, or more substantive work if the intern can't transfer their calls.

• Quickly learn your way around the campus (Capitol complex). Don't try to know all of it at first; just building locations, the Member's committee rooms, the cafeteria, the Members' Dining Room, and the House Floor in the Capitol.

• Go on a Capitol tour with somebody else to get a sense of how to take guests around the Capitol. Pay close attention, you're probably doing it next.

Not many staffers will offer assignments to interns who don't seem to be trying very hard. Usually, the quality of work you do on early will determine other work offered to you throughout your time with that office.

Whatever you make of your intern experience, it will be a rare experience for you to carry into the workplace when you leave college. References and letters of recommendation from a Member of Congress are a great addition to the portfolio of a young graduate scratching for a job after college. Take those things with you before you leave the Hill.

THE CAMPUS

Known by many staffers as the "campus," Capitol Hill has House office buildings along Independence Avenue across from the Capitol Building. They are named after former Speakers of the House.

Across the Capitol grounds are three Senate Office Building. The campus also includes the Ford building that houses support offices.

Interns need an official (but temporary) ID to access the Capitol, and get you to staff-only entrances when the lines back up outside the checkpoints. You will run errands throughout the buildings, taking letters for signatures or making time-sensitive deliveries.

Most spoken references to the buildings are by first name; most written references are the letters of the building:

• Cannon House Office Building has 3-digit room numbers. Two-digit rooms preceded by a "B", such as B74, are located in the basement of Cannon. The Congressional Identification Office is 321.

• Longworth House Office Building has four-digit room numbers that begin with a "1." There is a cafeteria, carry-outs, Office Supply Store, cleaners, and more.

• Rayburn House Office Building has four -digit room numbers that begin with a "2." It includes a first aid station, large cafeteria, two carry-outs, a Library of Congress satellite office, and many administrative liaison offices, all on the basement floor.

• The Library of Congress buildings include the Jefferson Building, the Adams Building, and the Madison Building. An intern is most likely to run errands to the Madison Building, which houses the Congressional Research Service (CRS) and a cafeteria/buffet. The Jefferson Building is the original building of the library complex, and houses a famous main reading room.

• The Senate office buildings include the Russell Senate Office Building (RSOB), Dirksen Senate Office building (DSOB), and the Hart Senate Office Building (HSOB). They are on the opposite side of the Capitol complex.

• Subways and tunnels: House and Senate office buildings, the Library of Congress, and the Capitol are connected by an elaborate tunnel system. Members and staff use these tunnels to escape the heat, the cold, and the tourists. Carry maps and diagrams around until you learn the place; obviously, maps won't help if you are in the tunnels.

OFFICE STAFF OVERVIEW

Members of Congress have several offices, one in Washington and one or more in their state. For purposes of phone messages and inner-office memos, you will probably see most people/offices referenced by initials.

• Chief of Staff supervises all staff work and is responsible for the overall management of Washington and District offices.

• Legislative Director is responsible for the Member's legislative portfolio, riding herd on the issues/committees under the LD's purview — as well as supervising the other legislative assistants as they negotiate issues, legislation and answer constituent mail.

• Press Secretary is responsible for all press releases, speeches, newsletters, and contact with the press or public (including social media), photography, and website maintenance.

• Legislative Assistants vary in number and experience, monitoring legislative issues and answering constituent mail. They handle specific issues, or committees, or agencies. Most offices have an "issue list" at the intern desks to help you direct calls to the right LA.

• Legislative Correspondent handles all issues relating to constituent mail, data entry and the data base, assigning new letters to LAs, and ensuring constituent's questions get responses.

• Staff Assistant is responsible for visitor services (Washington-area and Capitol tours, White House tickets, etc.), office reception, and routing of incoming calls and correspondence.

• Scheduler/Office Manager handles the Member's scheduling, gets anything related to office accounts, and manages the office generally (maintenance on systems, office supplies, etc.). All office deliveries usually go to the office manager.

• Technology Advisor advises staff on technology needs, does all installation/backup, runs systems and handles technical issues.

Often, offices will combine positions – or move around components of one job to another staffer – if somebody can handle more than one of the policy or administrative jobs.

TELEPHONE CALLS/DETAILS

For a generation more comfortable with texting, know that the right move is to answer the phone first, rather than hoping someone else will answer it. Answering phones is an intern's constant duty, even if you are working on something else.

The appropriate greeting is generally: "Good morning/afternoon, Congress(wo)man Name's office, may I help you?" A phone call may be the only contact a constituent ever has with the office; courtesy, tact and good manners are universally demanded.

Get the following information from a caller: correct spelling of their name, their organization, and the purpose of their call before transferring the call to the staff member.

Here's the dynamic for a staff member deciding to take a call ... maybe they have something to finish before they can talk, or don't have an answer yet for the caller, or a thousand other reasons for needing a message.

If the staff member wants a message, get the correct phone number, including area code, and read it back to the caller. Information in a phone message should also include the time, date, and should be transmitted quickly.

If you're not told the procedure for transferring calls to the boss, find out who those calls go through. Hardly any members take a call cold. And shouldn't.

The general script for calls goes something like this after you've answered it:

Caller: "May I speak to so-and-so?"

You: "May I tell them your name and who you are with?"

Caller: "Joe Blow with the thing in the district."

You: "Thank you, one moment please"

You dial the staffer and give them the caller's information ... and follow the staffer's directions.

Always have paper and pen to write with. Many calls come in at once and it is easy to get overwhelmed if you are not used to it. If calls are coming in too fast, use the hold button, saying "Congress(wo)man Name's office, can you hold please?" Go to the next line repeating that until phones aren't ringing, then go to the first line again, and go through the script.

Always use the hold button when you are not talking to the caller. Putting your hand over the mouthpiece means people can still hear you on campus phones.

Avoid putting your boss on hold.

Do not discuss the Member's position on issues, or offer your own opinion to the caller. In extreme cases, if somebody is enraged to the point they are abusive of you, or cussing … say something like, "Hey, I want to pass on your message, but please don't yell at/cuss at/berate me, I'm just an intern." That almost always works.

INTERN ASSIGNMENTS

Congressional office work can be challenging, monotonous, generally time sensitive, and interesting. Be resourceful in completing work assignments and ask questions if you do not understand the task. Ask what procedure to follow in order to complete a task.

Asking questions about how to do something means you care about getting it done right. Asking the same thing over and over means you are not paying attention or can't remember things.

SUGGESTIONS/HELPFUL HINTS

Lots of Members are informal and friendly, especially among staff, and some even tell interns to call them by their first name. Don't do that. They are elected, and Members deserve the respect of your using their formal title. Even if your Member insists on being called by a first name, only do that behind closed doors; use the title in front of people.

You are responsible for keeping a copy of signed letters or other documents that you believe is special work you produced in the office. These can be used as writing samples for future employers.

Particularly during the summer months, interns will have opportunities to attend lectures featuring prominent speakers. Don't assume you can be out of the office; notify your intern supervisor or the office manager that you want to go.

But do try to take advantage of all these lectures.

Capitol Hill receptions offer interns the chance to grab a beer and fill up on finger foods for supper – given interns are generally poor and trolling for food. They don't exist for you, so don't assume you may attend any reception you see setting up or hear about; ask your intern supervisor or the office manager if you can attend, see what they say.

Don't get drunk if you do get to go. Bad form for anybody … very bad form for interns.

3. GENERAL OFFICE INFORMATION

OFFICE HOURS

Hill offices are generally open 8 a.m. or 9:00 a.m. – 5:00 p.m. or 6:00 p.m. – know your hours, how to get time out of the office to participate in internship programs, and if that time must be cleared in advance by the intern boss. Get a number to call for if you are sick. There are no mental health days for interns. So actually be sick if you say you are. Hangovers don't count as sick.

Usually you have some time for lunch, and interns coordinate lunch times with the other interns and the staff assistant so phones are always covered. Get the rules of the road for your office in terms of lunchtime, where you can eat (generally not at the front desk) and if you can bring food from home.

GENERAL BEHAVIOR

Even interns reflect on the operation of the office and the reputation of the Member. Most offices demand courteous and respectful behavior with all office visitors.

The Member's personal office is usually off-limits unless you are invited in.

All office business must remain in the office ... more candidly, when you are out with other interns telling the legend of the day, don't tell stories out of school. If you don't know what that means, you shouldn't be in a congressional office.

People are listening everywhere: bathrooms, elevators, lines, the next table ... it's eerie who's listening to you and what gets back to your office.

If you get to sit in a meeting ... sit there and observe; offer not a word.

You are an intern. If you use the office kitchen, clean up what you mess up; your mama's not there. Also, nothing really needs to "soak."

Do not accept gifts on behalf of the staff or the Member; all incoming items for the Member go to the scheduler, or they are directed to a particular staff member – the HOR has strict gift rules.

Don't discuss issues with constituents – despite any inclination you might have to "teach" a constituent about an issue, refrain. Conversations should be as brief as possible ... get name, complete address, and the message ... if they say it's about such and such issue, make sure you get if they are for it or against it.

Don't ever talk to the media; don't post anything about your office on social media. Never.

If you ever say the words, "Oh, I just thought..." in conjunction with a decision you made, you've mucked up something and look really stupid.

There is zero tolerance of sexual harassment: from/by Members, staff, constituents, visitors, lobbyists – if anybody does something that makes you feel uncomfortable, go directly to your supervisor... they will make any decisions, take any actions from there. If for some reason they don't take action, there are other – way more serious – options. Pursue those through the Office of Compliance at http://www.compliance.gov/

Don't date the staff or other interns in your office ... the staff really ought to know not to date you. Nothing screws up an office dynamic like relationship drama.

When you are addressing any elected official on the phone or in the office, use the office holder's title and last name.

DRESS CODE

Get specifics from your office, but when Congress is in session, you should dress in an appropriate manner. That usually means ties and jackets for men. Women should wear something they can bend over in and not reveal the lady parts. Also, the chest should be covered, as well as the tattoos some adult once told you were a bad idea.

When Congress is not is session, some offices allow interns to wear jeans. Some do not.

OFFICE VISITORS

Office visitors – particularly constituents – are a priority. They should be greeted immediately and made to feel at home. Introduce yourself, talk to them, answer any questions and offer to be helpful. Immediately offer them water, coffee or whatever there is. Show the love; they vote and they talk to people.

CONSTITUENT MAIL

This is voluminous, and it is the lifeline of information to Members from constituents. It is also private and should be handled respectfully. Take great care in entering names and addresses for response mail if you work with the LC on data entry.

SCHEDULING

Refer all inquiries about the boss's schedule to the scheduler. If you have questions about the office schedule, ask the scheduler or staff assistant. You have zero information to share with callers or visitors about the boss's schedule. Even that he/she is in town can be too much information.

"I just don't know, but I can give your message to the scheduler." Even if you've given the same message to the scheduler a dozen times and the boss is dodging the caller, stay on the script. Again, "I'm just an intern" can frequently extract you if the situation gets tense.

COMPUTERS

Interns should not download any computer programs without the knowledge of the supervisor and the permission of the tech director.

Accessing any private web-based e-mail account from a terminal in the office becomes part of the permanent electronic profile, which can be subject to subpoena or review if office records are ever collected or requested. Obviously, that also holds true for an office email. Just use great judgment in all things.

ASSIGNMENTS

When you go to a staffer's desk to get information for an assignment, always take pen and pad. Keep a running list of assignments/progress ... for example, if you were asked to send out a letter, once you draft it, it's just drafted (it'll be edited at least once). Keep stuff on your list until the thing is done, or until somebody else specifically takes it up. There is no such thing as a stupid question; ask until you know what you're doing.

USEFUL DAILY READING

National Journal's CongressDaily AM and Congressional Quarterly's CQ Today (these publications list daily events, hearings, briefings, press conferences, etc.), plus the weekly Congressional Quarterly, National

Journal, and news websites in the district. Three Hill papers are also delivered daily during the week.

HOUSE ID

Your House ID is temporary. It is the property of the HOR and must be returned – don't be cute and "lose" it the last week. Offices can't get other IDs till that's resolved. Return the ID; you'll have other mementos. Interns losing IDs is one of the nightmare scenarios for Capitol Police, that's the easiest way for a bad guy to get easy access to the campus.

EMERGENCY EVACUATION

You might experience an evacuation drill – or an actual emergency evacuation – in your brief time on the Hill. Actual campus emergencies usually arise out of air traffic veering into restricted airspace. It's just over five minutes from detection to target, and the House will remove House leaders before telling the whole campus to evacuate.

So – at best – you have around four minutes to haul yourself from your desk to get outside; if it is an attack, you'll most likely still be in the buildings if you hesitate to go fast. If your office is on an upper floor or in the front of the building, in the first minutes, move to the side of the building away from the Capitol, then go down.

Very few offices spend time on emergency plans. Nobody wants to contemplate their own demise. There is no foolproof plan to get safely out; the best move is to get out very fast (in the opposite direction of the Capitol), and get to an off-campus meeting place. The buildings are filled with thousands of people. Confusion will be the rule; even among Capitol Police.

Most people will be in a little bit of shock in the urgent dump-the-buildings evacuations. So walk your route out at least once the first day or week you are on campus.

You will hear a fire alarm, don't wonder if you should leave; get up and head towards the door.

Try to stay with somebody from your office, but do not wait on anyone.

React to events ... if your way is blocked, be aware of other exits, and don't forget about using loading docks in the back of buildings.

Once outside, text your mother or family member to tell them there's an emergency evacuation going on, and you are outside the building. In an actual emergency, cell service will be spotty; don't panic, they move the grid to first responders.

Many offices simply take the plan the Capitol Police offer and plan no further.

In most events with an incoming bogie (errant plane), the Capitol Police have been confused at some level ... and thrown their own (orderly) plans out the window. The cops are human; and they cannot leave the buildings until staff is all gone – and after they have checked the building.

So if a bogie ever hits, we will lose a ton of cops still inside, clearing the buildings.

Most evacuations are a terrifying five or ten minutes, followed by hours of irritation that you got scared so bad ... and really furious at the dufus who violated the airspace.

FIRST DAY (generally speaking):

- Get acquainted with the office, buildings, staff, procedure
- Turn in ID card application in to the House ID office
- Learn phone system, start answering phones
- Fill out any paperwork for your office

FIRST WEEK (generally speaking):

- Learn more about office procedure, who does what, who gets what mail/questions, etc
- Get signed up for a CRS orientation course, if your office suggests it
- Learn Capitol tour
- Take many notes – from the first day on – to refer to so you are not re-asking stuff you have already been told
- Walk through the emergency get away
- Familiarize yourself with office computer systems

4. HILL SHORTHAND, ACRONYMS

Like any community unto itself, the Hill speaks its own language, complete with nicknames and a slew of acronyms. This little list is nowhere near the monumental vocabulary of Capitol Hill/governmental acronyms – or nicknames – but it does cover what's in this briefing.

Bullpen = the biggest room housing staffers in House offices

Campus = the Capitol complex

CBO = Congressional Budget Office analyzes economic issues and the budget process

Chief = Chief of Staff

CHOB = Cannon House Office Building

Comm Director or "**flack**" = Communications Director, Press Secretary

Conference report or CR = the final bill considered before signing into law

CQ = Congressional Quarterly, the morning daily publication lists events, hearings, briefings, press conferences, and covers legislative develops

CRS = Congressional Research Service

Dear Colleague = letters from a member to other members, tout legislation or causes

DO = District office

GAO = Government Accountability Office, the independent, nonpartisan auditors that work for Congress

Getaway day = the last day of the week your boss is in town, usually corresponds with last day of HOR votes

Hearing = members of a sub/committee hear witnesses talk about a bill

HOR = U.S. House of Representatives

House Action Reports = CQ's "bible" for offices every legislative day; offers factual breakdowns on legislation, floor summaries to highlight bill changes, and conference summaries laying out final bill language

House ID = the biometric photo ID issued to staff and interns

LA = Legislative Assistant

LC = Legislative Correspondent

LD = Legislative Director

LHOB = Longworth House Office Building

LOC = Library of Congress

Markups = when members of a sub/committee "mark-up" or change a bill

Member = Member of Congress, the formal name of the office in the House of Representatives

MRA = the pot of money for each House office annually

OM = Office Manager

RHOB = Rayburn House Office Building

SA = Staff Assistant

SOB = Senate Office Building

USS = United States Senate

This is just a tiny taste of the ocean of acronyms and Hill-speak. Every agency has acronyms, most bills and laws, movements … everything. CRS probably has a compilation of the most recent assortment of acronyms.

5. STAFF POSITIONS – OVERVIEW

Always remember who you are here – you're only the temporary helpers for the constitutional officers elected to serve in Congress. The staff isn't anybody special – but this is probably the most important, fulfilling, interesting work you will ever be chosen to do ... unless you are elected to office later.

WHAT NOBOBY SAYS ...

Once you start working on Capitol Hill, your time is no longer your own. Your life is really no longer your own. Offices usually pretend to carve out time for family; everybody wants to seem "family friendly." But your leash is always going to get yanked to deal with everything that might come up while you are not in the office.

The Senate might be better about that, but smaller HOR staffs make it hard to get out by 6 p.m. daily ... or for days-away vacations.

Know going into it that vacations, or any time away, is incredibly hard to schedule in a busy office. Congress is notoriously bad at missing self-imposed target dates for adjournment, even in election years.

Despite how adamant leadership offices are that business will be done by such and such date (called "target adjournment," or just before a "district work period"), that is almost entirely hopeful.

The money you will earn as a staffer is simply for crap in this expensive east coast city. That won't change. The only people with healthy salaries are those with very senior positions and tons of Hill experience, who could usually be earning several times their salary on the outside.

Salary will be a constant irritation and conflict ... for chiefs and members who must pay talented people less than they are worth ... and for young staffers trying to live in – or near – prime national real estate, pay back student loans, and eat ... and for more experienced staffers, who are also often supporting families.

Even worse, salaries are publicly disclosed. So the world will know what you've settled for ... to try to serve the public good. A chief once said, "The cheapest commodity on the Hill is brains."

Over the time of your service you'll toss plane tickets that you can no longer use because you bought them in advance, only to have vacations cancelled because the House has not yet adjourned.

That happens a lot, not because anybody is mean or out to get you. Most offices don't let staff leave for vacation if the House is in session. There are lots of good reasons for that, and nobody can tell you in advance exactly when that's going to be.

Ethics is ... well, a pain. Necessary, obviously, because past Congresses and staffers misbehaved ... or took expensive gifts in return for legislative favors. Nevertheless, that's the terrain that everybody must now live in. Get the briefing and follow the rules, scrupulously.

THE OFFICE DYNAMIC

Most offices are physically divided like this: a private office for the boss, a reception area, another small office (usually near the boss's office and usually occupied by the chief), and a bigger office generally known as the "bullpen."

The bullpen usually houses the biggest part of the staff, but every office slices space differently. Most congressional offices often bizarrely resemble a reality show, or a sitcom. Sometimes high drama ....

Congressional offices usually have smart, talented, opinionated people that sit practically on top of each other. Everybody hears everybody else's conversations, business or personal. It's usually a team of wildly different talents, all of them important to office operations. People thrown together like that either gel ... or they stumble a lot.

Congressional staffers need great attention to detail, while dealing with multiple issues and assignments. Staffers need to navigate the fast pace, and to move effortlessly between assignments.

The stress of finishing the daily crush of work can make you absolutely nuts, so much so that the House has on-campus counselors. Take advantage of them if need be, there will be days you feel like you are going a little bit insane.

Each day seems more like three days each. Sometimes it's like a ball machine is shooting balls at you to hit.

There's really no such thing as a lunch break. Keep trail mix, peanut butter, or whatever, in your desk. On some days, that may be all you can eat before late afternoon. On Mondays or Fridays there might be lunch meetings. Enjoy them.

In the community of people on the Hill, just in member offices, a good staff is one with a couple of veteran staffers with over a decade on the Hill. Everybody else is in their first or second job ... broke, usually wildly overwhelmed and trying to figure things out.

People have a tremendous capacity to grow. Some flourish in the atmosphere, many grow into it. Others run screaming from it, or stay just long enough to "stamp their ticket" – usually a year or more to make contacts and get minimal experience – then try to parlay that into a job earning much more money.

A Congress is two years, each year is a session. Once somebody has been on the Hill for two years, through both sessions of Congress, they've pretty much stayed until the end of the party ... which starts all over again with the next Congress.

If you want to know what's the least amount of time you need to put in to get the most experience out of it, it's two years – but has to be two years with a full Congress. Never leave your boss prior to elections. Very unseemly. To leave before an election, go before July begins, preferably earlier.

A reporter once said he never talked to anybody who'd been on the Hill less than a year ... he saw no need to try and develop a working relationship with somebody who might well be gone in a few months.

Again, don't date the staff or interns in your office. That's just a remarkably bad idea, and chances are that you are not the .001% of couples that meet in the same office and last. Somebody usually cries when it's over, then it becomes a huge distraction everybody else is gonna be mad about.

Interns are young ... they usually admire you, and are frequently attractive. Fight the temptation; be the grownup, however new that may be to you. Stay the hell out of their drama. Also, keeping a secret in a congressional office about fellow staffers dating is a nearly impossible feat, however clever you think you are.

There are staffers and interns outside your office. Hook up with them ... away from the office.

Capitol Hill is a small town, with everybody in everybody else's business. Gossip flies fast and furious ... about politics, legislation, individual Members of Congress, staff members ... whatever there is. Don't give anybody anything to gossip about.

Mostly, avoid the gossip – keep your eyes on politics and legislation, and whatever else you need to know to do your job.

TINY INSIGHT INTO MEMBERS

Members of Congress are usually a different kind of animal ... they are elected and they balance a ton of interests and considerations every minute of every day. They generally set the tone for how the office works.

Your boss isn't awful for blowing up in the office, at you or at somebody else. A Member has to be good-natured outside his/her office, all smiles, all that. Sometimes, the dinkiest thing is the last straw … and draws the loud ire of the Member.

They need to blow that off somewhere – far better politically if they do it in the office, among people on his/her side.

When you leave the boss's office or are finishing up a conversation with the boss, say "thank you sir – or ma'am" as you walk away. It's good manners and always ends an exchange with your boss on a respectful note, even if you just disappointed your boss, or vice versa.

When your boss – or anybody – asks you something you don't know, say "I don't know." Don't be one of those guys who try to bluff their way through it. You'd be surprised how many Members test staffers with something they don't know to see how they react.

Guessing ranks very low on what they want to hear. The right answer is: "I don't know. Let me find out."

Also, give Members their space. This will take some discipline, but stay the heck out of your boss's life. Give them as much personal space as is humanly possible. When your boss takes a call from the kids, spouse, significant other, or another personal caller – have the good grace to step away, give the boss an itty bitty little bit of space.

Members try hard (usually) to keep some level of a private life out of the office. But the office space is so intimate, the hours brutal, the work often exciting, and the team pulling together to hit a deadline is thrilling. Lives and private business get pushed out more and more. It takes a pretty heroic effort to carve out a life for yourself while always on call.

But it just takes a tiny effort to give your boss a little minute for a personal thing. Those efforts are almost always deeply appreciated.

CONTACT WITH CAMPAIGNS

Only a couple of people on the staff are legally permitted some level of interaction with the political campaigns – an office is not an extension of the campaign. Conceptually it is, but legally and logistically it is not.

Chiefs have the most discretion in contacts with the boss's campaign.

If it involves scheduling the boss's time, the scheduler is permitted to talk to the campaign.

If a reporter approaches the Member with a campaign-related question, the press secretary can talk to the campaign, talk to the reporter.

None of these specifics is a license for anybody else to "legally" talk to the campaign – on office time, or from the office, or using office resources (phone, computer) – so don't do it. If you really need to talk to somebody in the campaign, wait till you are outside your office and call from your personal cell.

Unless you've done this for a while, don't do any of that without reviewing the most recent rules.

DON'T WORRY

Now that you've heard candor about working on the Hill, you should also know that it really is a great job. When you leave, you'll feel a little lost. Or free ... depends on how much time you do.

Capitol Hill is a splendid prison, as is the White House. But it's not the "Hotel California" – you can check out and leave anytime you like.

The work is very cool, it's awfully important, and the people are some of the most interesting people you will ever meet. Every single day is different, or a little different

But nobody else will tell you, in such candid detail, about the essence of working on Capitol Hill. It is brutal. Just know that going in. The more you know in advance about expectations of you ... from the Member, the chief, the LD, and sometimes others ... the better prepared you are to handle the situations as they run over you.

ONLY CONSTANT IS CHANGE

Do not let your work – or your comfort level – depend on somebody else in the office. The only constant on Capitol Hill is change ... with revolving staffers mostly, but also in tone, ethics rules, majority party, technology, and nearly everything else.

Staffs being small, when one person exits and another enters, the dynamic of the office alters slightly. Get used to it. The only constant is change, and it will change a thousand times – for a host of reasons – in the span of a couple of years.

One of the best analogies about working on the Hill: it's like an ocean wave ... the only option is to ride it. Staffers who try to control it get crushed by it.

6. CHIEF OF STAFF

The Chief of Staff supervises all staff work and is responsible for the overall management of Washington and District offices.

If you are the chief, most likely you don't need this information. If you are new to the Hill, the job – or are looking for best practices – this might be a useful shorthand summary of the Congressional Management Foundation overview, the CRS briefings and leadership seminars.

The chief makes the final decisions on all office budget matters (although usually the office manager keeps the books, does the accounting and paperwork).

You are the law in the office, you are responsible for all hiring/firing/promotions (unless your Member wants to be more actively involved at that level – but that is almost always a universally bad idea).

You set the tone and are the "spear catcher" ... usually the deliverer of bad news and the one who must say "no" to friends and others. If it was an easy decision, it wouldn't get kicked up to you or your boss.

You already know your boss, his/her habits and preferences, the politics, the Hill and the district. If not, you are in way over your head ... figure out how to catch up.

HIRING

Hiring is a tricky thing; you are often entrusting very sensitive information to young and inexperienced people ... so be hyper aware of the importance of each hire. It is always a very bad idea to hire the iffy children of important political supporters.

Many offices wind up needing to do this sometimes, so carefully consider which portfolio they could do the least damage to. But remember ... that work will get doubled up on another staffer, or it will go undone –

and undermine the staff dynamic.

Hiring staff from the district is always the best idea ... but the other side of that is if you judge them wrong, or they just cannot keep up the pace or the excellence, you are stuck with that.

Or you have to fire somebody from the district ... somebody with family and friends who are voters and constituents, who talk to other voters ... somebody who might even mischaracterize matters to the local paper.

So tread carefully. Mostly, new hires are a gut thing.

Best practice is to hire staff members on a three-to-six month probationary basis. When staff members know what is expected of them from the beginning, and have a monthly conversation about issues, problems, process, or whatever ... they can know where they stand. Knowing they will be judged right away has a way of focusing a new hire's attention.

At three months, have a candid review of each staffer's work ... their successes and shortcomings. You ought to have a good idea by then if somebody's going to cut it or not; but they still have another few months to do it better.

At six months, let them know if they will remain with your staff, or if they are leaving. If it is pretty apparent they are not succeeding, even after the three month review, let that staff member know you will try to help them get another job ... maybe one that is better suited to their "talents." Those are awful conversations.

That's how most offices fire people, particularly if they are from the district. That also takes time and energy, to find a job for somebody that was misjudged at their hiring ... somebody who couldn't cut it on the Hill.

That exercise also inspires more consideration and vetting for each hire. Toughest hires:

• **Chief** (this is advice for the Member)
Only advice is find somebody politically smart – that you trust – who can administer a million dollar-plus budget, can adapt to developing situations, and who knows the ins and outs of both your district and Capitol Hill. Mostly, it's your gut.

Most Members take their top campaign staffer to be chief. Those are different talents (campaigning and chief-ing). Lots of those guys adapt and thrive on the Hill. Lots of others run screaming back to the world.

You'll have a good idea about your chief's progress as they deal with a staff ... and a better idea after the first month or so.

If it's not working for you, have the talk after the first month. Both of you cut your losses.

When it is working, let your chief hire and fire staff. Personnel crap is awful and distracting – you'll have plenty of that otherwise. At hiring, meet the top three candidates your chief vetted for you for positions.

Then stay the hell away from firing. That particular – hopefully rare – terrible job is for your chief.

• Legislative Director

This should be somebody who has done this for a couple of years elsewhere on the Hill (not a lobby shop), knows all the contours of committees and the entire two year congressional cycle. You need a workhorse, somebody really smart about how the legislative process can reflect your agenda.

Never take anybody's word they know the process. Get details from the other offices the candidate worked in ... and ask a series of questions about how to do stuff legislatively. That'll narrow it down if need be.

• Press Secretary

You need a workhorse writer, preferably somebody who knows politics, the Hill process in depth (most of their job will be explaining the process to reporters), who understands the dynamic of the news industry, and who knows their place. Sometimes it is a good idea to hire a reporter (TV, radio, or print). But not always.

• Office Manager

Find somebody uber-organized, reliable, pleasant ... mostly somebody to whom you are willing to trust with your office money, and access to the boss.

KEEPING EVERYBODY ON THE SAME PAGE

Hold a weekly staff meeting (Mondays are usually the best days), to go through the Member's schedule, legislative schedule, and whatever else is important to discuss as a team.

The art of a good staff meeting is brevity and staying on point.

It's important to have your staff write down what they are doing, not a book, just notes in a weekly memo to keep you, the LD and the boss updated on meetings, legislative progress and other matters of interest. Staff members frequently exit quickly and either don't leave a transitional memo (aka, "brain dump"), or leave a crappy one.

Some offices have the staff write "white papers" on each issue they oversee, with regular deadlines to update them.

Whatever works best for you, when a staffer leaves suddenly, a series of weekly memos or issue summaries can help reconstruct what that staffer was doing.

A lot of offices spend too much time trying to "reinvent the wheel" for lack of good information on recent events or actions.

Right off the bat, if you don't have one, create a staff manual to lay out the rules of the road – obligations, expectations, specific duties and responsibilities – so everybody is literally on the same page coming in.

The Congressional Management Foundation sells an office manual (off campus), or ask House Counsel's office/leadership office, somebody else in your delegation, or a committee colleague (all on campus) – to use theirs as a model to fashion one.

Some of these office manuals are heavy with legalese, others are more general instructions. Best advice, get guidance from House Counsel, but make a staff manual one with more general instructions.

Every office on the Hill is essentially its own nonprofit entity. There are some basic House rules, applicable laws, and ethics obligations to ensure staff conforms to Hill policies from the outset. Don't harass or discriminate based on age, physical disability, race, color, religion, sex, marital status, orientation, or national origin.

There's not a judge and jury, or Labor Relations Board; the Hill's generally exempt from all that.

You have the Ethics committee; and an office of compliance ... which "does not impose uniform workplace practices, such as work schedules, job duties, salaries, vacation and leave policies, holidays, fringe benefits, or procedures for hiring and firing staff" (from the handbook of the HOR Office of Compliance).

There's generally one employee in Member offices (usually the front office staffer) that is "nonexempt" in terms of hours. Past that, other things are the specifics of your office.

So that's the universe of considerations in hiring or firing staff. You can't violate civil rights or abuse people based on circumstances (overwork or being underpaid does not count as abuse on the Hill) ... but if you stay inside whatever the House Counsel says is the bright lines, your boss – and you – are the absolute law there.

Work on the Hill is "at will" – that's at the will of the Member. Somebody's perfume irritates you, you have the authority to fire them and they have little to zero recourse. But ... find another reason to use.

PAYING THE BILLS

In the House, the MRA (Members' Representational Allowances) is the pot of money allowed for each office annually. Offices must use it without going over. There is no room for going over. If that happens, it comes out of the boss's pocket.

It must pay for everything related to the office and congressional representation: travel, lodging, equipment, salaries – everything.

If your office manager is brand new, best advice on use of the MRA is to use a shared employee for budgeting and accounting, someone familiar with the House ethics rules ... and the multiple rules and nuance associated with the MRA. You'll be saving yourself a huge headache and lots of bad press on gambling that a rookie employee can catch up on all that.

With a shared employee for MRA matters, an office can combine Office Manager with scheduling and staff assistant duties, save a little money on a salary.

When possible – when you are confident your office manager has a strong handle on the myriad of MRA rules – best practice is for the office manager to handle the MRA.

In most offices, the chief has the office manager run the MRA, keep financial records in order, and get information for the chief on budget, MRA questions or budgeting scenarios.

PROCTOLOGY REPORTS (DISCLOSURE)

Your boss and some staff are required to regularly disclose information about financial, travel and other office-related matters through the Clerk's Office.

Your office manager generally rides herd on these reports for the office … keeping up with coming deadlines, providing information and forms, usually with a checklist of everything due by a time certain.

You want to sit with whoever is handling the disclosure to go through statements and other components of what is needed, for the boss and probably for you.

Staff required to make disclosures are usually determined by salary, so the first time you do it talk to the Clerk's Office or House Counsel to make sure your office is touching all the bases, doing it right.

Some of the information the office must regularly disclose:

• financial information (source, type, amount, and value of the outside incomes),

• foreign travel paid for by HOR (usually with a committee),

• franked materials (samples and descriptions of mass mailings to your districts),

• gifts and travel (paid for by someone else) and charitable contributions to House members, officers, and staff,

• any legal expense fund,

• and a couple of others that don't apply to most offices – but when doing this for the first time, check the clerk's website to see if anything else applies to your office.

Bear this in mind as you are compiling or reviewing disclosures: reporters back home are going to have a very good time at your expense, so stay in front of whatever might be politically embarrassing or surprising for whomever.

GET AWAY BOOK

Member briefing books are a handy tool for your boss, and utilize the traveling time well. Format is whatever is easiest for your boss, and should be in his/her hands or on the tablet well before leaving for the week on "getaway day," the last day the HOR votes, or before the boss leaves town or leaves the office.

Contents are whatever your boss might need for the time out of DC – from releases and remarks ... to letters and memos, maybe reports, bills, coming schedule ... whatever your boss would want in it. Usually the LD or Press Secretary will compile this weekly.

HISTORY OF ACCOMPLISHMENTS

Every office keeps an "accomplishments list" that lists every single thing the boss did that year. There is more detail about this in the press secretary section; the list is usually compiled regularly by the same staff member – whomever you would choose.

It is an excellent resource for your campaign. Share that carefully. If you post it on your site, even for a while, it becomes public domain ... but make sure you are inside the current rules as you do that.

SIGNING DOCUMENTS FOR THE MEMBER

Capitol Hill has way too many staffers who substitute their judgment for yours – maybe bypass the approval process, go straight to the Member. Sometimes that will be the process. All to say, have a process and follow it every time, so you avoid mistakes in letters, press releases, or whatever.

In establishing that, make sure there's an alternative to your final approval if you get stacked up. Most offices use the LD as a backup for the approval process ... this includes designating an office "signer" for letters or other documents that need your boss's signature when he/she is out of D.C., unless the Member wants to sign everything personally. Then it becomes a scheduling matter.

ETHICS CONCERNS

Ethics is such a pain that some Members keep a lawyer on the side for incidental questions on House Ethics matters ... to get an answer in advance, see the contours of the law on the particular thing they are asking about.

If you ask Ethics anything, you're on the record asking. Asking for guidance in advance of Ethics helps you hone the "ask." More than one lawyer has described the legal needs of Capitol Hill as "can-I-do-it?" law.

"I didn't know that" isn't just a lame excuse anymore; it's now an infraction unto itself. Get the Ethics briefing. It's required. Listen carefully and stay clearly on the right side of the law.

When there is EVER a question about "I wonder if we can do whatever" ... call the lawyers. You'll be surprised what is and isn't acceptable.

A little truth... and you'll hate this: when somebody offers to pay for supper, or offers you a little gift ... say "no thank you, I got special obligations to consider. I hate that, and I thank you, but no."

You will serve the government far better if you accept nothing. That will also make you unusual.

Many offices do a bunch of events with outside organizations (a business procurement conference, veterans benefits conferences, seniors' events, etc.) – and there are very strict rules that govern how offices can operate with outside partners in those activities. There are generally a lot of letters, brochures, website content, etc. for these events. Someone on your staff must go through them all with Ethics or Franking Commission to determine what is permissible.

The Ethics Committee governs how Members' offices can (but mostly cannot) work with outside organizations. Best advice is to call the lawyers at Ethics to ask a specific question about the specific event.

Ethics training is mandatory; get it behind you ASAP. Bear in mind, you're no longer breaking rules that could embarrass your boss politically ... you are now also avoiding breaking a law for which you could serve jail time. Bottom line, stay above reproach.

INTERNS

Interns are the luck of the draw and are nearly always unpaid. Office managers usually choose, brief and babysit the interns, although that varies all around.

Offices usually have a relationship with a couple of regular intern programs from which to draw interns. Mostly, kids will find you. Best if interns are at least sophomores in college.

First thing to tell prospective interns is: internship is unpaid. Sometimes conversations stop there. But offer up a spot in the DO when that's a problem. Do not get caught up in issues with intern housing/transportation. Have a general memo to interns who will be in your office, with info on housing/transportation/navigating D.C.

You gotta both protect interns – and kick them around a little bit. Remember, they are college kids who have usually – but certainly not always – been pampered all their lives and are pretty sure they know more than you.

Have an intern manual (House Administration Committee usually has information on intern housing and a manual you can adapt for your office) – that should go through how your office works, what you expect of interns, and your rules of the road.

Whoever briefs interns will be best served by a list to read from in the first meeting with interns, so that everything gets said up front.

Regularly remind the staff not to date the interns and not to socialize with them individually. That's a hard call to make – obviously staff members get close to interns, and generally offices invite them to receptions. But it is awfully bad form for staff members to date interns – or each other for that matter.

Don't expect more from interns than they are capable of giving. Again, they are temporary college kids. As their internships wind down, their head almost always goes to the next thing. Don't be disappointed.

Their level of talent/promise will cover a wide range … from wildly talented … to pretty good … to useful for tours but not much else … to stinkers … and – who you should try to avoid – the lazy children of the rich you get stuck babysitting.

When asked for a letter of recommendation for an intern, have the interns draft their own recommendation. It's usually pretty entertaining … and interns will have a better memory of what all they did in your office. All need to be edited very heavily.

TECHNOLOGY NEEDS

The technology advisor makes recommendations to the Member, chief and staff on technology needs, does all installation, runs systems and handles technical issues.

The best practice on hiring tech directors is to use a shared employee, an outside vendor who is an expert in House IT communications, who takes care of IT needs, installations, purchases, new system research, security, general advice on data extrapolation and website functions, and other IT platforms and programs.

Those things have such specific and unique ramifications on offices, ethics, budgets … it's always best to have an expert running the bases. It's cheaper and more reliable than hiring somebody specifically for IT in your office.

Many offices use the House Information Resources [HIR] Office technology representatives for tech support. While HIR services are free to offices, the reps may not be able to respond quickly to office needs, particularly during the busiest legislative seasons, when you need it the quickest.

Given that technology evolves hourly, the office needs – and House rules governing technology – will also evolve frequently. Talk to several other offices to see how they run their shop, and decide how to organize tending to your office technology needs.

But the database itself in each office is maintained by the legislative correspondent – or another permanent staff member that the chief designates. Whichever way you choose to address the office technology needs, the office data base is generally maintained by a permanent staff member – almost always the LC.

7. LEGISLATIVE STAFF

The Legislative Director/LD is ultimately responsible for the Member's legislative portfolio, riding herd on the issues/committees under the LD's purview – as well as supervising the other legislative assistants as they negotiate issues, legislation, pass on vote recommendations to the boss, and answer constituent mail.

The general shorthand for legislative staff is "legis" (pronounced LEDGE) staff.

From time to time it will suck to be you, just because you are responsible for other people's work (the other Legislative Assistants/LAs and the Legislative Correspondent/LC) you supervise.

FLOOR NOTEBOOKS

When your boss's committee has a bill on the floor, Members are generally there for most of the debate. Floor notebooks should include different sets of remarks (rule, general debate, various amendments) and any props (i.e. a letter or chart) that the boss may want to wave around or refer to if he/she needs to rebut something or underline a point in floor debate.

The art of any of these notebooks is brevity and usefulness to the boss.

COMMITTEE NOTEBOOKS

The staffer for your boss's committee/s nearly always prepares notebooks for all subcommittee and committee meetings/hearings. They include background memos, draft remarks, questions for witnesses, witness bios, hearing background, stuff like that ... most of which will come from the committee.

GETAWAY BRIEFING

This is a brief your boss carries out on getaway day (the last day of HOR votes, or the last day on the Hill before the boss takes off), so start preparing it early in the day and putting stuff aside for it all week.

As always, it will vary from Member to Member on preference, digital or hard copy ... and types of things in them.

Goal is not to load them up; some might be big, most shouldn't be big at all. Each one is different, but basically each one might contain:

• Press releases/HOR remarks from the week.

• Remarks/mood music for an event that weekend.

• Any draft remarks down the road, not necessarily for the current weekend.

• Any legislative briefs (many times legis staff will update the boss with memos or briefs).

• Reports that are important or interesting/topical (always highlighted).

• Schedule for the coming week.

• Anything that the boss hasn't had time to read but probably should read (stories, constituent mail of note, etc.).

Members spend lots of time travelling so this is a really good use of the transit time to get briefings on matters that were not high-level-urgent over the past week, but of note to the boss. Although, a better use of travel time for members is to sleep ... there's so little of that anyway and it generally improves minds and demeanors.

CONSTITUENT MAIL

This is the cross for every office to bear; it never ends. It's the best communication between your boss and the people back home. But for you, constituent mail will be a constant ... there are always new letters to write, older letters to update, and new letters to draft/edit/plug in the database.

In a week when every single minute seems to have been taken up with meetings, hearings, or monitoring the Floor, constituent mail usually falls to the bottom of the pile. Most offices have a deadline for responding to an inquiry (not drafting a response, but actually responding).

So many LAs need the weekends/evenings to write constituent letters.

Constituent mail brings an array of responses. It's everything from easy questions, to nuanced policy questions, to correspondence with multiple questions to address across issue lines.

Every veteran office will have a wide variety of general and specific letters addressing topics and questions. Most letters are automatically answered with pre-written letters ... but every day brings a different kind of issue, and requires new letter text that must be updated or drafted, then vetted and proofed.

Sometimes the leadership offices will have a menu of sorts for constituent letter drafts, and you can take that and specify it to your office needs.

Be creative with your time as you are running to grab lunch, or in a hearing, or on Metro, to draft constituent mail. Otherwise you'll be writing it all weekend. Or be very far behind the next week.

When – not if, but when – the constituent mail responses fall behind, make the following weekend a mail party. It's not so much a party as it is requiring all staff, even non-legis staff, to be in the office on Saturday to work exclusively on constituent mail catch-up.

If legis staff know in advance that particular anvil is hanging over their heads, they might find other ways to fit in drafting letters during the week.

LEGISLATIVE ASSISTANTS

Legislative Assistants (LAs) vary in number and experience, monitoring legislative issues, meeting with constituents, and answering constituent mail. They handle specific issues or agencies. As early as possible, get the CRS briefing on the legislative process, and any party leadership briefings.

MANAGING INFORMATION

Don't be overwhelmed by the tsunami of information pouring into each congressional office. Everybody and their mother will try to persuade your boss to vote with them on matters ranging from dinky to monumentally important.

You can never read everything that piles up on your desk.

If your boss is consistently conservative or liberal in their votes, that's much easier for you. Find the most reliably ideological (one-sided) information to follow, to justify your boss's stands on particular issues.

The best information will be from CRS or the CQ backgrounders. Unless you need a purely ideological resource to rely on, you can toss nearly everything else that piles up on your desk. Keep anything from the district or the state. If your boss is intellectually curious – or middle of the road – give your boss both sides of the argument to make the best decision on votes.

MANAGING TIME

This will depend largely on your routine, how you work best. The LA workload includes research, writing legislative memos (almost daily), writing update memos for your office (probably weekly), writing constituent letters (which is a constant crush), following legislation, and sitting in meetings, hearings, etc., all of which eat up lots of time in the day.

The bulk of the writing (memos, notes, committee remarks, witness questions, etc.) is best done in the morning early from home, or late at night in the midst of a busy legislative season.

No matter how inefficient any Congress is, or is portrayed, Congress gets judged on final action ... getting legislation passed and signed into law.

Congressional staffers, however, are usually even busier in unproductive sessions just because there are a greater number of negotiations, new proposals ... and high-level strategy sessions that seem to never end, with a mad dash to define to the press what the Member is doing.

LAs are never caught up; the best you can do is be a few days behind.

Always keep a running list of tasks/assignments; it's useful to move stuff to a "done list" to use as a basis for a weekly update.

Every week, an LA should synopsize the week's activity in a memo to keep the LD, chief, and the boss updated on the week's meetings, legislative progress and other matters of interest. If it is a heavy week, it might go over a page, but otherwise keep it as short as possible.

Too long a memo only means you're looking to justify how you spent your time... a concise memo means you are busy and working hard.

FOLLOWING/NAVIGATING LEGISLATION

There is a weekly schedule out early every week that lists most scheduled legislation coming to the floor that week.

Committees of jurisdiction or the general subject matter usually determine which LA handles which issues. The LD makes all bill assignments, usually at a legis staff meeting early in the week.

Daily legislative schedules list the bills up that day and that week. Before legis staff meeting, an LA should have read pertinent background on the bill and all amendments that are expected; Rules Committee almost always lists amendments. Votes on rules prior to bill consideration are almost always party line.

Your boss will want to know the following about upcoming bills/amendments:
• Sponsor,
• Associated cost,
• Effects on district/state,
• Previous votes on similar legislation or issues (last thing you want to do is get your boss flip-flopping),
• Some Members like to know how other Members of the delegation are voting,
• Most Members want to know how the party leaders plan to vote (or

chairmen and ranking Members on committees),
- And the pros/cons coming from both sides.

Often, the disposition of amendments will determine how your boss will vote on final passage.

When you have a bill on the floor – or a hearing or markup – schedule meetings around it and carefully monitor the whole debate. Taking a call and missing what happened will make it look like you cannot do several things – proficiently – at the same time.

Many times those things will all crash together at the same time – no amount of planning can make that any better.

Most legislative staff will "hand off" monitoring duties if they absolutely have to leave to take a call or meeting. Point is: if it is your bill, you are responsible for following the process from beginning to end.

At the same time, usually meetings are scheduled in advance and bills come up on the floor willy-nilly. Be monumentally creative about how to use your time. You won't have much of it.

Often the House – on busy days – will vote in clusters, so frequently there will be a series of votes to line up for your boss. You never tell your boss how to vote. You make recommendations only. Your boss casts votes – and runs for re-election – not you.

There are probably Members who never ask for vote recommendations, but do ask their staff for all pertinent background.

Give the recommendations or background to your boss before he/she gets to the floor to vote.

The hardest part of all legislation is the end game – the "conference report/CR" – or the final bill. It is a good idea to ingratiate yourself to the committee staff for your party, somebody you can call and get inside information when you need it. If you develop such a relationship, do not abuse it … and they will know what you are doing.

Committee policy staff is the "elite" corps of Capitol Hill staff. They are very smart.

THE LEGISLATIVE SEASON

The busy hearing schedule will be winter-March, the heavy full committee markups are around May. June and July are very busy – consistently long days – right up to the August break. Then September through adjournment is conference reports … a lot of hurry up and wait … getting party members on board with whatever, futzing what the Senate has done (or what the House has done) to legislation.

Making laws is a very arduous process, as it should be. Normal rules would have the Congress passing the final version of the 12 appropriations bills, but increasingly, Congress passes bills to fund the military (and whatever else they can get in it) and fund the rest of the national bills in a single "Continuing Resolution" or "CR" to keep paying bills/obligations and servicing the debt. Then the bickering is over how much to trim the CR.

It is a pretty insidious way to run a government that has a pretty careful process … but many times, Congress passes a bill in the House – and an altogether different one in the Senate – but then never passes the conference report (the final bill negotiated by Members from both chambers).

So they can say they voted for this bill in their chamber, but stood up to whatever the other chamber did … and they fund the government/service the debt in a giant spending bill that nobody ever reads.

It's a gargantuan bill, and many times the final bill is only available to read as the bill comes to the floor. That's why there's a week or so worth of embarrassing stories after they hit a deadline … and rush to pass a bill nobody's really read in its entirety, besides the staff that hurriedly pasted it together to please 218 Members of the House of Representatives.

That's the magic number: 218, which is the majority of 435 Members in the House. Watching the scoreboard on floor action, know that when one side reaches 218, that's a majority.

But never report the final results of a vote until the gavel has fallen and the chair announces the score. All too often, a final push by one side or the other can sway enough Members to change an earlier outcome of a vote before time runs out.

INTRODUCING LEGISLATION

Don't worry, you're not writing it… an LA would normally get direction from the LD up front. LAs will write a memo about it to Legislative Counsel (under the Clerk's office), describing what the boss wants the bill to do – and Legislative Counsel produces the legislative language. There is usually a little (or a lot) of back and forth on the language to perfect it to your boss's satisfaction.

Some Members want "original co-sponsors" of a bill at introduction – mostly to show some level of support for it. Your boss's signature must be on the bill, as well as on any list of co-sponsors, and delivered to the House floor.

Co-sponsoring bills is a good, low-maintenance way for a Member to attach his/her name to legislation that reflects the Member's political sensibility or common purpose. Troll through Dear Colleague letters daily to find any bills that your boss might be interested in.

SIGNING LETTERS, BILLS, OTHER DOCUMENTS

Some Members want to be the only one who can sign their name. If that is the case with your boss, your game will be to get the letter/legislation/whatever to your office while the boss is there and has time to get to it.

Most offices have a designated signer to get on letters and such, for when the boss has seen the text and given permission, but is out of the office.

APPROPRIATIONS vs. AUTHORIZATION

A common early mistake for Hill staffers is misunderstanding the difference between appropriations bills and authorization bills.

The actual process for legislation is: one committee must "authorize" money for something, and another committee must "appropriate" or spend money for whatever it is. In that process, authorization committees have the first whack at a bill, and then hand it off to the appropriators.

The chairmen of all the appropriations subcommittees are nicknamed, "college of cardinals" (after the cardinals leading the Catholic Church) … illustrating the absolute power they have over all Congress' spending decisions.

Just know when you read a bill has "authorized appropriations for…" it is the authorization bill. "Authorize" would be the key word.

The spending of money is always – only – done through appropriations bills. The committee of jurisdiction is also an indicator. If the bill is not a product of the Appropriations Committee, it's an authorization.

MEETINGS

Meetings with constituents or interest groups can sometimes take forever. There is an art to shorter, efficient meetings. Obviously, show the love to constituents; in scheduling, they should get preference because your time is limited.

The crux of nearly all meetings with advocates is: what is it? How much? Why? Who's involved? The meeting's not really over until you know the answers to those questions.

Ninety nine percent of constituents want to meet with the Member. Meeting with the LA alone is so settling for second (or third) string. On busy days, many offices have the staff meet with the constituents or interest groups to get the gist of what their request/legislative interest is … and have the Member drop in.

The drop in is to say hey, take a picture and get a fast update from the

LA, and hear anything else the visitors can get in before the Member has to duck back out.

Many visitors bring something in writing … a letter to your boss or background on the thing they are talking about. When you go to the meeting, be sure to ask for that first … and ask them to give you the :30 second overview (preferably without reading the information itself). If you can get the info first so you know what's coming, you can shortcut the meeting a lot and go directly to questions or follow up.

Meetings should never go over 15-20 minutes.

Never, ever commit your boss to whatever the visitors are advocating for. If you do make a commitment, you need to go get elected so you can do that. Bear in mind, you have no idea the myriad of other commitments your boss has made, or what other considerations he or she has at a given time.

USE OF CRS

CRS exists to do the hard research. If it's something you can't research online – or have an intern research it – then consider going to CRS. But don't waste their time with dinky crap. They have a ton of updated research on all topics.

BRIEFINGS FOR DISTRICT VISITORS

Offices frequently have other Members or distinguished guests from other states visiting your district. Offer them a short briefing of logistics, schedule, local staff contact in the state, recent articles on the thing that brings them there, suggested bullets for remarks (if you are asking them to speak) a simple overview, and whatever else would be necessary to know.

The shorter these are, the more likely they are to be read – it should not be a book, more like, "Just the facts, Jack."

ANSWERING CONSTITUENT MAIL

The LC handles all issues relating to logistics of constituent mail, matching up incoming mail with current responses, data entry for new contacts/outgoing mail, assigning new letters to LAs, and ensuring constituent's questions get appropriate responses.

You'll be almost dizzy at first at the tonnage of incoming contacts.

Tough place, this is usually the most junior legislative staffer, but is often charged with overseeing the logistics of the letter progress of more senior LAs. The LD usually is the editor – and the police on LAs getting letters finished.

The process can get bottlenecked with an LA backed up with other stuff, not getting to a draft ... or with an editor backed up with other stuff.

If at all possible, draft a letter for an LA, or some part of it, to move it along as far as you can ... but don't ever assume letters go out with only your approval.

For the LC, what matters is the turnaround time from getting a contact ... to answering it. An LC should be creative about getting letters going, keeping the process moving around constantly.

If you are a new LC, familiarize yourself with the files of letters in your office to get a rough idea of what letters currently exist, so you won't be writing something you've already got a draft for.

The task of data entry will fall to you, not interns (although they can help, and you need to spot check the work pretty regularly), and not anybody else. It's crazy tedious and it never stops.

But you maintain the database. If you do that badly, chances are you won't move up in the office and will be moving on pretty quickly.

USE OF INTERNS

Interns will vary in their writing ability, but many offices will test an intern with having them research a little issue and write a letter to respond to it. Give them a letter or whatever to model their assignment on, so they will see the intro, the rhythm of requested information, and the letter close.

Sometimes interns can be very helpful this way. The downside to interns is that they are always temporary, and sometimes don't put the attention to detail to get a good draft to an LA, or follow the process to the moment something is actually sent out of your office.

DIRECT MAIL

While the LC conducts the daily logistics of constituent mail, somebody else (usually the LD) often puts together a calendar of chase dates (Veterans Day, monthly holidays or anniversaries) and overlays that with a schedule of mailings that will hit topics cleverly.

Direct mail differs from constituent mail because direct mail is unsolicited.

There are rules about how many "unsolicited" responses an office can send, and the office pays all postage out of their MRA (the pot of money for each House office).

There are usually also several direct mail follow-ups to constituents who have contacted you about a bill/issue previously. Sometimes offices will send out updates to constituents who asked about a particular issue when further action is taken or completed.

8. COMMUNICATIONS OPS

The essence of being the Press Secretary/Communications Director is to be aware of what is happening throughout your offices, what needs to be pitched as news stories, what's coming up policy-wise and event-wise, what the office should and shouldn't respond to, what stories are percolating, and how to be part of them.

There are several duties for most Press Secretaries:

• everything press-related (including writing press releases about everything Congress is doing, how it affects the district, statements or reactions, coming up with ideas to generate press, talking to reporters, pitching stories to reporters, prep for press conferences, etc.),

• (usually) all speech/event preparation,

• writing all publicly read letters,

• unofficial keeper of history/accomplishments per session,

• website and social media content, and

• designing and writing any postal-delivered newsletters (these are so unpopular with everybody except congressional offices), and e-newsletters.

The most important trait of political communications is the ability to understand not just how to say things well, but an intimate, nuanced understanding of how they will be heard; to see around the corners, know what's coming up; knowing how to utilize opportunities before and as they come up, and always bearing in mind the boss's point of view from logistics to politics to policy and historical context.

The press secretary usually advises the boss and the chief on the overall communications efforts of the office. Your boss is perfectly capable of directing the press ops. Your job is to offer your best advice. If you don't have advice, shut up … or say "I don't know."

In-district stuff and state stuff is priority. If a local paper and the *Wall Street Journal* or the *Washington Post* both call, call the local paper back first.

BE A GOOD SOURCE

Press releases are the most frequent means of putting out news from your office ... and it's important to make them as useful as you can for reporters. That includes saying – in simple words – the essence of the news in the lead ... useful quotes from the boss ... any pertinent history about the issue and your boss's activity on it ... and what must happen next for action to continue or be finalized.

Being a useful source also includes sending them out by 4 p.m., at the latest – it's better to send them out before that, although often news breaks later in the day. That means the draft, the legislative review, and getting a release in front of your boss for approval all has to happen long before 4 p.m. Any one of those steps could get hung up and last an hour or more.

The clock ticks on... and the press secretary is one of the few people in the office with daily deadlines set outside the office.

Bottom line, if something's going out late, it's after stories are written, long past when reporters will start a story or include your stuff. So dance around as it gets late. As the afternoon goes on, begin to evaluate if somebody else (somebody in the district, somebody else in the state delegation) will go out with this news before the next day, maybe it'll hold over. Obviously, big, breaking news is different.

Don't be offended when stories from releases are never printed with your slant on a story. Sometimes smaller pubs will run them in their entirety – and that's the reason to make info in a release as complete as possible – but reporters digging out stories will take releases as news tips.

That means they will likely call you for fresh quotes, call the guys on the other side of whatever it is for their take ... follow with questions and write a story from that.

Your first stop after you get off the phone with a reporter is the desk of whoever's handling the issue, or the LD. Get their direction, which may be to kick it to the chief or the boss at that point ... but it may also glean you info about a meeting, or bill, or letter with recent action that day or week that might be topical for the story.

An important thing to remember in terms of getting press: talk about what they're writing about. If you know a reporter's working on a story about X and you are doing a release on Y, either relate Y to X ... or put out separate statement on X. If you know what they're writing about, try to get in that story.

Letters your boss sends to other officials make excellent – and easy – news releases. A lead, text of the letter, and a closing graph makes it easy.

Never know when one of these makes news.

Everybody thinks they know how reporters think (ironically, they think reporters would see things from that person's point of view). They are almost universally wrong. To know how reporters think, you have to be one. To get just a little insight, you have to talk to them every day.

Be good natured about it, but know that when people yabber on about how reporters think – unless you know that they have specific insight you don't have – don't lean on that advice. Always listen to the little common sense barometer in your head.

When your boss attends a public event back home, drop an advisory prior to the event so it will be listed on area daybooks. When a news organization gets an advisory, they don't need to be covering that event ... but might just come for a chat with your boss on another story.

It's good to add an FYI after the when/where/what in an advisory, such as, "this week the House added whatever to a thing that my boss cares about; she/he is happy to talk about that."

"NEVER ARGUE WITH PEOPLE WHO BUY INK BY THE GALLON."
-- Yogi Berra

Hard part about talking to reporters is the "thinking forward," for lack of any other term. When talking to reporters, if it's tricky ... or you don't know a lot about a subject ... or just practicing safe flacking ... slow down the pace of what you're saying to think forward to judge how what you're about to say will be absorbed, what questions could result, and where that could take the conversation.

All to say: think before you talk, and particularly while you talk ... which is much easier said than done. But it's a very handy tool to develop; most people don't start out with this particular talent.

Your whole role is to be helpful to reporters while delivering your boss's message without getting sloppy ... on letting out info that could turn the conversation to a topic off point.

Remember what reporters need and how their days run ... they need information they can attribute that's of interest to the community (but first of interest to their editors); they need good concise background (not heaps of reports, unless they ask for that; and some will); they'll need fresh quotes from sources; and they need to turn in multiple stories a day.

So, giving them as much info as possible and understanding their needs goes a long way in helping them understand your perspective, and that usually gets reflected in their stories.

Never, ever get in front of the boss when talking to reporters. Part of a reporter's job is to charm you, make you speculate about what is going to happen. That's very dangerous territory. When you get to the end of whatever you know, say that.

The most frequent phrase for you in initial conversations with reporters should be, "I don't know ... let me find out and get back to you."

Remember, when you're talking to a reporter ... if your name appears in the story the next day, it will be followed by your boss's name.

It's not uncommon to get sick at your stomach when talking to reporters at first, or after a dicey conversation.

Keep your name out of the news if at all possible. You are never the story. Only one person in your office is elected ... everybody else is just helping out for a while. In fact, when a reporter asks how to spell your name, ask if they can just quote a "spokesperson for" your boss. That name is the only name that matters.

Some "don'ts" ... don't EVER lie to a reporter. Be charming, be funny, go completely the other way ... if something's absolutely going south, hang up if all else fails (gotta go, bye). But don't lie. It's like being a virgin. The single failing will always haunt you, and you may never even know it. Reporters talk, be utterly aware of that ... and it all reflects on your boss.

If for some reason you are ever told to lie to a reporter, make sure your boss and the chief know what comes after that ... the least of which is nobody will ever believe your boss, make the boss a joke.

Ever hear the phrase, "The cover-up is worse than the crime?" Lying to reporters about something that is brewing that is bad for your boss, only makes it worse. Depending on what it is, it could be about some activity policed by the ethics committee or the local district attorney. Also, in this situation, look for another office to land in.

Don't be smart-alecky ... be respectful of reporters ... their jobs, their challenges, their workload ... their toil in pursuit of the First Amendment. They not only have the right to question you, it's their responsibility. Remember to cherish that, no matter how screwed up it'll get.

Reporters have a constitutionally protected suspicious nature. Nothing is ever truly off the record.

Prior to hooking your boss up with a reporter, put any pertinent info in front of him/her, a release, a story the reporter is looking for response to, a report about something ... none of which will be useful to the boss at that point unless it's highlighted.

Every Member will have a unique way of going about talking to reporters; figure it out and how you can be helpful to your boss.

Always put yourself in reporters' shoes (particularly as you are walking the boss to a press conference), anticipate what the hardest or obvious questions will be, share that thinking with your boss. That way even if it's tricky to answer, the boss will be kicking it around in the back of his/her head, and won't get caught cold.

If you need to tell your boss something while he/she's on the phone with a reporter – write it down and put it in front. But wait till he/she ends their thought before showing a note. Otherwise you trip up your boss's rhythm.

Talking to somebody while they're on the phone is very distracting. If others are trying to talk while your boss is on the phone with a reporter, end that quickly; get them to write it down.

EXCLUSIVES

Two sides of the coin on "exclusives" from a congressional office … you get good coverage from one news source that one time. But every other news outlet/competitor will be awfully mad and less likely to use info you give them in the future.

There's a way to play "footsie" with reporters to break a story without exclusive stuff from your office. But tread carefully there too; if it's that big, go to the AP, which is your "one stop shopping."

Your worst day will be the day you make a smart aleck or smarmy remark to a reporter and it winds up in the paper, embarrassing your boss … or getting ahead of the boss on saying something to a reporter about a matter he/she hasn't made up his/her mind about yet.

Deliberation is mighty important, and giving your boss room to do that is a healthy part of this job. Don't hint at an eventual position on a thing at all for a while, then only sparingly and only if you are absolutely certain.

WHAT HAVE YOU DONE FOR ME LATELY?

The accomplishments list reflects the history of legislative and other accomplishments for the year so the boss and staff have a ready history of what happened … how much money the boss got for this and that.

It's a huge doc that you draft, using press files as a guide.

Helpful advice: draft this doc in one sitting so you don't lose your place. Best done on a weekend, and after the last funding bills have been passed for the session. Go through every single press release, lifting the meat of it into the accomplishments doc. On grant releases where there are two or more funding announcements (such as SBA money to two separate entities), that becomes two (or however many) lines in the accomplishments list.

Bear in mind this document might eventually become the underpinnings of a political doc to tell voters what the boss did in the previous year/Congress, guide how the campaign phrases stuff in political documents.

Best to divide it by appropriations and policy … and you only use the appropriations number from the final appropriations bill. It would be awful to shout one number, only to have the entity in the district, with specific knowledge, publicly correct you with the lower number.

The policy side is going to be the far heavier side of the accomplishments list. Once you have a good draft, move it along to the LD for info from the legis shop that may not have been in a press release … then to anybody else on staff that contributes before this finalizes and goes to the chief or the boss.

MORNING NEWS CLIPS

Most press secretaries scan websites for the boss's name in news stories (so many people use news alerts that an early morning search might catch stories you've not gotten an alert about yet) and email the Member, chief, and the pertinent legislative staff, any stories with the boss's name in them. Most Members like to read these stories very early in the day while there's time, rather than on the run later in the day… although there'll be plenty of that, too.

Most district offices have a compilation of news clips from local newspapers they send up early in the day.

TELEVISION

TV is nearly always the preferred mode of information, and local TV news needs are simpler than print reporters. And harder.

Easier because you know ahead of time their day … most reporters get in about 9:30-10a, get first assignments, go cover first assignment, go to lunch, go back to newsroom, cut from first assignment, be in line for second assignment, be done by 4 p.m., when they are back in newsroom editing stories, and getting final budget for evening news at 6 p.m. and 10 p.m.

For context, a typical local TV newscast has 19 minutes (or less) of air time for stories; subtract four minutes for sports, four minutes for weather … and actual news has just over 11 minutes of air time in a traditional 30 minute broadcast, essentially four-five stories, plus anchor reading. That's generally the universe of time you're competing for inside a local newscast.

So for TV, you plan appearances early in the day (if anybody asks you, 10 a.m.-noon is ideal planning time for an event). Be cognizant that if you can't get back to a TV reporter well in advance of their air time, your boss isn't in the story.

Don't call a TV station just before they are going on the air unless you have very big news … what they would consider very big news.

Challenge for TV is to make the story simple enough to be a TV story.

Budget deficit stuff is not a very good TV story, unless there's a letter from your boss to some honcho about it saying it'll keep money away from this and that in the district. That's not a bad story ... but probably not one that would make the cut without another hook (like a related study, accident related to it, something like that).

Frequently, TV stations want get your boss's thinking on a thing from D.C., and will do a "phoner" – a conversation either live or taped (taped is usually better for a Member, no forced schedule for the boss).

Phoners are a phone call a TV station can run on the evening news with intro, picture of the boss and sound from the taped interview. But it is TV; their preference is live or moving pictures.

A "live feed" is a little more involved, and takes getting a Member to a studio near the Hill to get hooked up and talk to a local anchor/reporter. These are very expensive for local stations, but they are invaluable communications tools. Republican Members have a little easier time getting into national stories with Fox News as a platform.

Local TV news is usually far harder to get into. And it is usually what your boss will want the most.

SPEECHES

Most Members have a nuanced process to prepare for public events, and a specific way they'd like any advance work done. Some Members will speak extemporaneously, some from notes, and some from text on paper ... many have moved to tablets.

Since there are at least 535 variations on a specific product, the following is merely one way to organize this.

The speechwriter wouldn't call a contact for an event for research unless it's certain your boss will be there. It's not solid unless the boss has agreed to go. Don't jump the gun, and call an event planner if it isn't solid ... they get excited he/she's coming and the disappointment will be worse if they think their Congress Member is coming – then does not.

Read the invitation, and then call the contact for the event. The first questions are confirming logistics, which are probably in the invitation: time, location, nature of event, and precisely what your boss's role is (keynote, welcoming, introduction of somebody, etc). Past that, you are usually looking to get:

• A draft program, most hosts won't have an official program until it's printed just before the event. All you need is an unofficial rundown or draft program, whatever they can give you to illustrate how the show will run. Many are as simple as pray, pledge, introduction, your boss speaks ... if so, say it thataway.

• Who will be on the podium.

- Who's introducing your boss.
- If they want to hear anything special included in his remarks.
- How long your boss should speak.
- If the press has been advised. Either way, ask if they mind if you put out an advisory; people hardly ever mind, but get the right event contact name to put in the advisory.
- If there is any background to include … about the organization, maybe from a web site or about the thing they are celebrating or focusing on.
- What VIPs are in attendance … and most organizers will not have RSVPs from everybody invited, so usually best to ask for VIPs invited/if any are confirmed.
- Get a contact name/cell number for day of contact … usually, but not always, this name is different from the contact name on your advisory. This is for if the boss is headed to the thing and just can't quite find it … or has questions at the last minute, or needs to let them know he/she is running late, etc.
- Always close these conversations with: "anything else you'd want the Congress/wo/man to know?"

Once you have all that information, put together a prep memo with just that info in it (the memo is something that should set the tone for how the event is supposed to go). It should be as short as possible.

The second part of the prep is message, which could be more like mood music or bullets, or a more formal speech. It's hard to write for someone, to be inside their head, to say just the right thing to the particular audience he's addressing. But that's the goal, to find just the right things to say, just the right way to say it.

Every style is unique; figure out your boss's. Run a draft by whoever best knows the issue, to make sure the sweet spots are touched, and to ensure the style and message are on target before it goes to the boss. Every office's editing process is different; every office's final product is different (some probably don't use written prep/speeches).

You'll always be well served to think through logistics from the boss's point of view …from getting there, to message, to delivery, to materials that will serve him/her best in advance … all that.

But also be creative … for instance if the boss (or a district staffer) is going to a meeting and there's some recent report about subject matter of note, send that along to give to the organization as an FYI, show the love.

The more quality information your guys in the district have, the better they can operate. CRS reports/GAO/IG reports are the most useful.

PUBLICLY READ LETTERS

When the boss can't make an event in the district, it is a good idea to send district staff to the event to represent him/her. They are often asked to speak on behalf of the boss. Rather than have them make up stuff willy-nilly on the spot, the best practice is to have them read a short letter from the Member if they are asked to speak. Then the DO staffer can hand it to a reporter ... maybe you'll make a story.

But no staff member should give speeches in the Member's stead; if anything, they should only read a letter. Remember, it's ALWAYS entirely about the boss, never the staff.

NEWSLETTERS/DIRECT MAIL

Postal newsletters are almost ancient now, but mailings will be some element of direct communication, at least for the near future.

Postal newsletters need approval by the House Franking Commission and must be in line at the printer's place well in advance of the mandatory cut-off date for franked mailings (be especially cognizant of this in election years).

Here's a little information intended to terrify you ... should an office ever miss the pre-election mail cut-off deadline, the Member is required under House rules to pay the entire cost of the mailing from his/her own pocket ... not the office budget, not campaign funds.

Typically, the cost is tens of thousands of dollars. So stay well in front of the deadline.

But before putting together your first one, review the many, many rules from the Franking Commission for size, subject for pictures, frequency and usage of name, personal pronouns, all that. The Franking Commission has a pretty complete layout of rules and a checklist for you to follow.

These newsletters are barely-disguised advertising, so you're putting your boss's name in front of people as they throw away their junk mail. Since it is badly-disguised advertising, the law requires this language on these mailings: "Prepared and mailed at taxpayer expense."

Estimate is: you actually reach about two or three percent of the people to whom postal newsletters are sent... half of which love you, half of which hate you. So even in the people you actually reach, you make little-to-zero headway.

While spam nets can block e-newsletters, you still gotta throw away the postal one, so printed materials travel through a voter's hands for the .5 seconds it's advertising your boss (while the voter is muttering "what a ... waste of money").

Nevertheless ... many offices still use this mode of communication, but members are best served by carefully targeting audiences (vets, teachers, unions, businesses, seniors, young people, military families, etc.), but that can be tough to get good mailing lists for.

The only useful thing to consider in preparing these – in terms of raising up the low retention average – is to include a story people will see as they are tossing junk mail (so must be visible in the top third of page one) that will be a useful resource for them in the comings days or weeks.

Example of that is as hurricane/tornado/storm season approaches in late spring … get in front of that with a newsletter featuring an extensive checklist if a weather disaster hits. Find an idea that would work best for your guys, something they might need.

ELECTRONIC NEWSLETTERS

E-newsletters are the preferred format since they are cheaper than old-fashioned postal newsletters. But they must also pass muster with the Franking Commission.

The very best way to get your boss in newsletters is to piggyback on other regular newsletters, or trade publications. If your office doesn't have a column in other publications, reach out to local chambers … or a shipping column in a stevedore's newsletter, or offer a column for a veterans' newsletter, or talk about economic trends in a business newsletter – you'll see other opportunities.

9. OFFICE ADMINISTRATION

Some chiefs will combine one or more of these portfolios into one staff position in Hill offices. Likewise, pieces of any portfolio (legis or communications) tend to move around, as staff talents, needs and time will dictate.

OFFICE MANAGER

Office managers, in short, keep the office running, no matter what.

The office manager is usually responsible for the Member's scheduling, gets anything related to office accounts, and manages the office generally (travel, payroll details, postage for outgoing mail, equipment purchasing and maintenance, inventory, office rent, office supplies, paying bills, etc.). All office deliveries usually go to the office manager.

In many offices, while the chief makes all decisions on budgeting/office accounting, it is the office manager that keeps those records in order, gets information for the chief on questions about budget and MRA (Members' Representational Allowances).

The MRA is the pot of money allowed for each office annually. Offices must use it without going over. If the office goes over their allotment, it comes out of the boss's pocket.

Some offices use a shared employee for budgeting/accounting, someone familiar with the House ethics rules ... and the multiple rules and nuance associated with the MRA.

Best practice – with a rookie office manager – is to use a shared employee for MRA matters and combine office manager with scheduling, maybe even front office duties. If the office manager has substantial Hill experience, and dealt with MRA previously, you don't need a shared employee.

The office manager tracks staff vacation schedules and balances (although permission for taking vacation generally comes from the chief or LD). You also manage commuting (Metro) benefits, the student loan program offered for offices, and ensure staff complies with the yearly ethics requirement.

Whether you write it or not, you will organize having an office manual with the specific office rules – from office hours to a Family/Medical leave policy, to emergency planning, and making sure each new staff hire knows to read it.

DISCLOSURE REPORTS

The boss (plus some staff) is required to regularly disclose information about financial, travel and other office-related material through the Clerk's Office.

The office manager generally rides herd on these reports for the office … keeping up with coming deadlines, providing information and forms.

These are detailed and you should compile a checklist of everything due by a particular deadline.

See what disclosure documents you need to get to staffers, and what documents you need. Catch the chief first to go through information to include for the boss and the chief.

Staff required to make disclosures are usually determined by salary, so know who is required to disclose in your office.

Bear in mind as you do this: reporters back home are going to comb through this, check the accuracy and write stories about it. Even something just sloppy will be a huge pain for your boss back home and in the press. Make sure the press secretary knows when it is public; the office will get press calls about it.

Some information the office must regularly disclose for the boss:
• financial information (source, type, amount, and value of the outside incomes),
• foreign travel paid for by HOR (usually with a committee),
• franked materials (samples and descriptions of mass mailings to your districts),
• gift and travel (non-HOR travel paid for by someone else) and charitable contributions to House Members, officers, and staff,
• any legal expense fund,
• and a couple of others that don't apply to most offices – but when doing this for the first time, check the clerk's website to see if anything else applies to your office.

SCHEDULING

Whoever does this component of staff work (almost always the office manager) will be fielding requests for time with the Member of Congress, getting breaking updates to the boss, pushing a scheduling meeting with the boss to go through the piles of requests, getting House or committee schedules and updates, making travel and accommodations reservations, updating passports … anything that pertains to the logistics planning, and time with the boss.

Some offices locate the scheduler in the D.C. office, some in the district office. Some even divide the scheduling duties, but that usually works out badly. Best practice is to have a single staffer managing all scheduling. It probably works best in the D.C. office, but lots of offices have schedulers located in the district.

All offices have their own practice of organizing the boss's time. But generally, when the scheduler gets a request for a meeting, you are initially looking for the following:

• Time/date/place of event or meeting request, or if it is at the boss's convenience,

• If it is an event, who is sponsoring,

• Topic of event or meeting, and any legislation they want to discuss, and

• Who will be involved in the meeting.

The thing you will say most often is "no" … so say it sweetly, with empathy.

You are always passing on a message, it's not your decision you are announcing. Do not get ahead of your boss with a hint that the Member is available for something, or that he or she might not want to meet about something.

Unless a scheduling matter is last-minute-urgent, or a special person stops by unannounced, best practice is to have a weekly scheduling meeting on a regular day.

Schedulers have to be aware of all the moving parts of a member's schedule … their hearings, markups, and days the House will consider bills important to your boss. Know how much time to block for those things. The LD is probably the one to ask about time on the House Floor … or time a committee/subcommittee meeting will consume.

Some of that can get futzed in weekly staff meetings. But it will mostly be on the fly. A little context, you are not so much in charge of the schedule as it is in charge of you.

Markups at the committee or subcommittee level usually take the most time out of a day.

Be creative with your boss's time ... for instance, if the boss is in a committee hearing, or voting on the House Floor, many offices prefer to take a meeting or constituent drop-by to the hearing room, or to wherever the boss is. He/she can step out, say hey, and duck back in.

Don't be offended if your boss dreads your scheduling meetings ... it's likely got nothing to do with you. It's almost a subconscious thing ... the Member almost thinks that by avoiding you, he/she can avoid adding more stuff to the already full schedule.

Try to make the scheduling meeting as painless (that means fast) as possible. Some schedulers (or other staffers) use the time on the drive to the airport do go through scheduling things. Safety tip, if you're the one using the drive time for a meeting, don't be the one driving.

Also, running possible meeting requests by the chief first, or another veteran staffer, can be very useful for you in advance of the scheduling meeting.

Some members trust their chiefs to make decisions about schedule, and only kick matters up to the boss if the chief has a question about a matter.

Always know where your boss is. Have several ways of finding your boss – including all the phone numbers ... plus the spouse's personal cell, and – if they have adult children – have their contact information as well.

TRAVEL

You will make all the travel arrangements, so it's important to keep credit card information and airline phone numbers with you at all times. Occasionally, the spouse will travel with the Member, so you may be entrusted with a personal credit card number.

You will have the most contact with the spouse – so make sure you have a good relationship with him or her. Be aware of birthdays and anniversaries, and any family events that may conflict with official events.

Keep a running list of every trip the boss takes. You'll need this for disclosure purposes. For overseas travel, have a checklist to make sure you have all the components the boss will need (passports, visa, background, etc.)

CAMPAIGN

It is also your job to make sure the campaign has time on the Member's schedule, and to schedule time to make campaign calls. Most members find "dialing for dollars" a loathsome duty at several levels. It is. But it is also the mother's milk of the political system, so it's important to press every week if you want your boss back in Washington after the next elections.

You are the office historian in terms of how the boss spent his or her time. Make sure you keep a copy of the final schedule each week. Somebody may need it to refresh memories about when a meeting occurred and who was there, or a thousand other reasons.

STAFF ASSISTANT

The staff assistant operates visitor services, office reception, organizes the flying of flags for constituents over the Capitol, and routing incoming calls and correspondence.

Basically, the staff assistant runs the front office and must be organized, pleasant, and quick on his or her feet.

The phones are constantly ringing, and the mail never stops. Constituents and other visitors are walking in early for appointments – or late for them – and sometimes are not on the schedule. Or an old friend of the boss will stop by. Or a high official will run by before a hearing for whatever. Or constituents come by thinking they are meeting with the boss, but are meeting with staff (on those, let the staffer for the meeting deliver that bad news).

A member of the boss's committee might run by to lobby for something; maybe the boss would like to dodge them for whatever reason.

All of that is just a little sampling of the multitude of people that can wind up in your front office.

So the staff assistant is part diplomat in terms of negotiating tickets and other things for the office, greeting the delivery guys alongside the high government officials, constituents, and other Hill staff … part babysitter for interns … and part security for the office, keeping everybody out of the bullpen (where the legislative staff works) and certainly out of the chief's/boss's offices … while charming all the guests.

Visitor services include sending out information on D.C.-area places of interest and frequently getting tickets to various buildings and departments around town.

Most popular tickets are White House tickets, and each office is allotted a certain number per week, but only if they are specifically reserved. Names on tickets must match the reservations made by offices, and the visitor's ID. Tour requests are made online.

You are only allowed to request tickets if you have the names and personal information of all the guests.

It is also possible to use a "Member Pass" that allows a certain number to come with the Member; those requests are also made online … and takes a couple of hours out of the boss's day, so this becomes a scheduling matter.

But never depend on the boss having a couple of hours in the middle of a busy legislative day to take visitors to the White House. There will be times the Member will want to go, or grudgingly go, but the busy legislative season is also the busy tourist season.

The staff assistants e-mail each other to try to find a way to get their constituents into the White House on Member-led tours. Have a good understanding of the current operation in terms of getting White House tickets. They frequently change.

Particularly in the summertime, the White House ticket requests are way more than offices can accommodate. When people are disappointed at not getting to see the White House, many offices offer a personalized tour of the Capitol with an intern.

Along with the office manager, the staff assistant is part of the administrative side of the D.C. office.

DISTRICT STAFF

The district staff generally includes: a District Director (who runs the district operations for the Member), caseworkers who handle certain agencies and certain specialties (such as veterans, Medicare, etc.), and sometimes a district office has someone dealing with special projects or grants opportunities/economic development in the district.

Have great respect for what they do … the district offices are where the rubber meets the road in terms of representative government.

ABOUT THE AUTHOR

Cathy Travis worked on Capitol Hill for 25 years as a communications director, senior advisor and political consultant for various Members of Congress until her retirement to be a full time author.

A native of Jonesboro, Arkansas, Travis graduated from Arkansas State University and resides in Washington, D.C.

Her first book, the award-winning *Constitution Translated for Kids*, was hailed by partisans in all major political parties as an even-handed, non-ideological rendition of the founding U.S. document.

Travis has been a registered Independent since March, 2001.

www.travisbooks.com

Other books by Cathy Travis:

Remember Who You Are (a novel): From a Capitol Hill confirmation hearing, Judge Jodie Davis – a nominee to the U.S. Supreme Court – tells the U.S. Senate about her childhood in northeast Arkansas in the turbulent South of the late civil rights era. The lives of young Jodie's neighbors are thrown into turmoil – first when a black family tries to buy a house in their neighborhood, then by a monster tornado roiling through their town. But none of that prepares them for the chaos in the aftermath of a murder on the football field of the high school. The decisions that everyone makes in the aftermath have enormous consequences for each one of them.

Elected (a novel): Inaugurated after a bitter recount in Florida, following the 2000 presidential race, President Hal Cord leads an angry and divided nation. White House Press secretary MJ Bennett watches in horror as her country is brutally attacked, and careens into a Central Asian war that threatens the life of her new love, a legendary Special Forces commander.

After September 11, 2001, Cord calls for a creative "worldwide war." Sending an overwhelming military force to Afghanistan badly damages Osama bin Laden's force there; and Cord's focus on eliminating the combustible engine forces al Qaeda to morph quicker than the group had planned, with dangerous results for Saudi Arabia … and the United States.

Target Sitting is a heartbreakingly candid journal written when Travis was a Capitol Hill staffer. Beginning the week after the September 11, 2001 attacks – *Target Sitting* carries readers through that heart-pounding day, the anthrax attack on the Hill, and the full body shudder associated with working at the seat of government in the ensuing years. *Target Sitting* is a stark look at life in the target that al Qaeda missed in 2001.

Constitution Translated For Kids – winner of the 2011 Gelett Burgess Children's Book Award for Education (Government and Politics), the "Mom's Choice Award" and a "Best Books Award" – is a simple, widely acclaimed, non-ideological translation of the entire U.S. Constitution, side-by-side with the original 1787 text. Teachers hail the accompanying free Teacher's Guide, and a Toolkit as extraordinary resources to offer lessons on Constitution Day in September.